STEP-BY-STEP

Sensational Salads

Sensational Salads

CAROLE HANDSLIP

||| •PARRAGON• |||

First published in Great Britain in 1995 by
Parragon Book Service Ltd
Unit 13-17
Avonbridge Trading Estate
Atlantic Road
Avonmouth
Bristol BS11 9QD

ISBN 1 85813 666 0

Produced by Haldane Mason, London

Printed in Italy

Acknowledgements:
Art Direction: Ron Samuels
Editor: Joanna Swinnerton
Series Design: Pedro & Frances Prá-Lopez/Kingfisher Design
Page Design: Somewhere Creative
Photography: Iain Bagwell
Stylist: Rachel Jukes
Home Economist: Carole Handslip

Photographs on pages 6, 20, 34, 48 & 64 are reproduced by permission of
ZEFA Picture Library (UK) Ltd.

Note:
Cup measurements in this book are for American cups. Tablespoons are assumed to be 15 ml.
Unless otherwise stated, milk is assumed to be full-fat, eggs are standard size 2 and pepper is freshly ground black pepper.

Contents

First Course Salads

The first course of any meal should be tantalizing to the taste-buds and not too heavy, so salads fit the bill perfectly. They provide an infinite variety of taste, texture and colour and a superb opportunity for the cook to display an imaginative flair and get the meal off to a good start by pleasing the eye as well as the appetite.

Use pretty dishes to complement your chosen salad: scallop shells for example, or other interesting shapes; or perhaps glass plates, which can be plain, coloured, decorated or frosted. Take care over the decoration and garnish, and use sprigs of fresh herbs where possible. Serve a first course salad with Melba toast or with one of the many exciting Mediterranean breads available, which are flavoured with oils and aromatic herbs. These are particularly suitable, as they can be served warm, in satisfying chunks, attractively served in a basket.

Opposite: Use the freshest vegetables in contrasting colours for a striking effect. Vivid reds and greens are particularly effective.

STEP 1

STEP 2

STEP 3

STEP 4

ARTICHOKE & PARMA HAM (PROSCIUTTO) SALAD

A pretty salad with a piquant flavour. Use bottled artichokes rather than canned ones if possible, as they have a better flavour. Basil has a warm pungent aroma that blends particularly well with tomato.

SERVES 4

275 g/9 fl oz bottle artichokes in oil, drained
4 small tomatoes
30 g/1 oz/¹/₄ cup sun-dried tomatoes, cut into strips
30 g/1 oz/¹/₄ cup black olives, halved and stoned (pitted)
30 g/1 oz/¹/₄ cup Parma ham (prosciutto), cut into strips
1 tbsp chopped fresh basil

FRENCH DRESSING:
3 tbsp olive oil
1 tbsp wine vinegar
1 small garlic clove, crushed
¹/₂ tsp Dijon or Meaux mustard
1 tsp clear honey
salt and pepper

1 Drain the artichokes thoroughly, then cut them into quarters and place in a bowl.

2 Cut each tomato into 6 wedges and place in the bowl with the sun-dried tomatoes, olives and Parma ham (prosciutto).

3 To make the dressing, put all the ingredients into a screw-top jar and shake vigorously until the ingredients are thoroughly blended.

4 Pour the dressing over the salad and toss well together.

5 Transfer to individual plates and sprinkle with the basil.

PARMA HAM (PROSCIUTTO)

This Italian ham is first dry cured and then matured for about a year. Once it is dried it can then be sliced very thinly and is served raw. It can be found in most supermarkets and in Italian delicatessens.

STEP 1

STEP 2

STEP 3

STEP 4

SEAFOOD WITH TOMATO VINAIGRETTE

Packets of frozen mixed seafood are now available, which makes this spectacular salad very quick and easy to assemble.

SERVES 4–6

1 red (bell) pepper
2 tomatoes
350 g/12 oz packet mixed seafood, defrosted and well drained
few sprigs of dill
lemon slices, to garnish

TOMATO VINAIGRETTE:
2 tomatoes, skinned and finely chopped
2 tsp tomato purée (paste)
4 tbsp olive oil
1 tsp wine vinegar
1 garlic clove, crushed
salt and pepper

1 Cut the red (bell) pepper in half and remove the seeds. Lay the red (bell) pepper halves cut-side down on a grill (broiler) pan and cook gently under a preheated moderate grill (broiler) until blackened.

2 Put the (bell) pepper into a plastic bag to cool, then remove the skin and chop the flesh roughly.

3 Cut each tomato into 8 wedges and place in a bowl with the (bell) pepper and drained seafood.

4 To make the vinaigrette, put all the ingredients in a bowl and whisk together.

5 Pour the vinaigrette over the seafood and mix thoroughly.

6 Arrange the seafood salad on individual plates, sprinkle with dill sprigs, garnish with lemon slices and serve with Tomato Toasts (see page 12).

SEAFOOD

If you cannot get hold of frozen mixed seafood, buy the fish individually from the fresh fish counter. Use a mixture of prawns (shrimp), raw squid prepared and cut into thin rings, and mussels. The mussels should be cleaned and cooked for 4 minutes before being removed from their shells. A few poached scallops cut into pieces would make a really special addition.

STEP 1

STEP 2

STEP 3

STEP 4

MEDITERRANEAN (BELL) PEPPER SALAD

Colourful (bell) peppers fried with courgette (zucchini) and onion are marinated in balsamic vinegar and anchovies to make a tasty starter. Serve with fresh bread or Tomato Toasts (shown on page 11).

SERVES 4

1 onion
2 red (bell) peppers
2 yellow (bell) peppers
3 tbsp olive oil
2 large courgettes (zucchini), sliced
2 garlic cloves, sliced
1 tbsp balsamic vinegar
50 g/ 1 ³/₄ oz anchovy fillets, chopped
30 g/ 1 oz/ ¹/₄ cup black olives, halved and
   pitted
1 tbsp chopped fresh basil
salt and pepper

TOMATO TOASTS:
small stick of French bread
1 garlic clove, crushed
1 tomato, skinned and chopped
2 tbsp olive oil
salt and pepper

1 Cut the onion into wedges. Core and deseed the (bell) peppers and cut into thick slices.

2 Heat the oil in a large heavy-based frying pan (skillet). Add the onion, (bell) peppers, courgettes (zucchini) and garlic, and fry gently for 20 minutes, stirring occasionally.

3 Add the vinegar, anchovies, olives and seasoning to taste, mix thoroughly and leave to cool.

4 Spoon on to individual plates and sprinkle with the basil.

5 To make the Tomato Toasts, cut the French bread diagonally into 1 cm/¹/₂ inch slices.

6 Mix the garlic, tomato and seasoning together, and spread thinly over each slice of bread.

7 Place on a baking sheet, drizzle with the olive oil and bake in a preheated oven at 220°C/425°F/Gas Mark 7 for 5–10 minutes until crisp.

BALSAMIC VINEGAR

Balsamic vinegar is made in and around Modena in Italy. It is made from grape juice concentrated over heat and is fermented slowly in wooden barrels. It has a sweet-sour flavour, but is rich and mellow and you only need a teaspoon or two to give a dish a real zip – which is just as well, as it is rather expensive.

PALM HEART & PAW-PAW (PAPAYA) VINAIGRETTE

A really impressive first course, in which the colours complement each other as do the subtly intriguing flavours. Use either the Lime & Honey or the Chervil Dressing.

STEP 1

SERVES 6

1 small paw-paw (papaya), halved and
    deseeded
400 g/13 oz can of palm hearts
1 bunch watercress
2 tbsp pine kernels (nuts), browned.

LIME & HONEY DRESSING:
grated rind of 1 lime
3 tbsp lime juice
2 tbsp olive oil
2 tbsp clear honey
salt and pepper

CHERVIL DRESSING:
2 tbsp caster (superfine) sugar
1 tbsp boiling water
2 tbsp chopped fresh chervil
2 tbsp olive oil
3 tbsp lemon juice

1 Peel the paw-paw (papaya) thinly and cut lengthways into thin slices. Arrange on individual plates.

2 Drain the can of palm hearts. Cut the palm hearts diagonally into rings and arrange over the paw-paw (papaya).

STEP 2

3 Break the watercress into sprigs and arrange around the edge of the plates.

4 To make the Lime & Honey Dressing, mix the grated lime rind and juice with the olive oil, honey and seasoning to taste.

5 To make the Chervil Dressing, mix the sugar, boiling water and chervil together, then mix in the olive oil and lemon juice.

6 Pour a little of the dressing over each salad and sprinkle the pine kernels (nuts) over the top.

STEP 3

PAW-PAW (PAPAYA)

The skin of a paw-paw (papaya) turns from green to an orangey yellow as it ripens, and should give slightly when pressed. When you slice one in half, you will find bright salmon-pink flesh with a mass of little grey seeds. The seeds are edible but are very hot and peppery. The flesh is delicious served simply with lime juice, but blends extremely well with other tropical fruits, or with smoked meats.

STEP 4

STEP 1

STEP 3

STEP 4

STEP 5

PEAR & ROQUEFORT SALAD

The sweetness of the pear makes it a perfect partner for radiccio, which is sharp, and rocket (arugula), which is peppery. The Roquefort dressing completes this wonderful marriage.

SERVES 4

60 g/2 oz Roquefort cheese
150 ml/¹⁄₄ pint/²⁄₃ cup natural yogurt
milk (optional)
2 tbsp chopped chives
few lollo rosso leaves
few radiccio leaves
rocket (arugula) leaves
2 ripe pears
pepper
chopped chives to garnish

1 Mash the cheese with a fork and blend in the yogurt gradually until smooth, adding a little milk if necessary. Add the chives with pepper to taste.

2 Break the lollo rosso into manageable pieces. Arrange on individual plates with the radiccio and rocket (arugula) leaves.

3 Quarter and core the pears, and cut into slices.

4 Arrange some pear slices over the salad on each plate.

5 Drizzle the dressing over the top and garnish with chives.

LETTUCE

If you buy lettuce that is not pre-washed, prepare it carefully. Break off and discard the outer leaves and any damaged leaves. Rinse the lettuce carefully and either pat dry with paper towels, or spin in a salad spinner, or wrap loosely in a tea towel (dish cloth), gather up the loose ends and swing it around – simple, but effective! It is best to do this outside, as some water will leak through the cloth.

ROQUEFORT CHEESE

A blue cheese from the southern Massif Central in France, Roquefort is creamy-white with blue-green veins running through it, and has a strong flavour.

If you prefer, you can cut the Roquefort cheese into cubes and add it to the salad leaves (greens) with the pears and pour a herb vinaigrette such as the one on page 15 over the salad.

STEP 1

STEP 3

STEP 3

STEP 4

SMOKED TROUT & APPLE SALAD

Smoked trout and horseradish are natural partners, but with apple and watercress this makes a wonderful first course. I like to serve this dish with Melba Toast.

SERVES 4

2 orange-red dessert (eating) apples, such as
*   Cox's Orange, quartered and cored*
2 tbsp French Dressing (see page 8)
¹/₂ bunch watercress
1 smoked trout, skinned and boned, about
*   175 g/6 oz*

HORSERADISH DRESSING:
120 ml/4 fl oz/¹/₂ cup natural yogurt
¹/₂–1 tsp lemon juice
1 tbsp horseradish sauce
milk (optional)
salt and pepper

TO GARNISH:
1 tbsp chopped chives
chive flowers (optional)

1 Slice the apples into a bowl and toss in the French dressing to prevent them from browning.

2 Break the watercress into sprigs and arrange on 4 serving plates.

3 Flake the trout into fairly large pieces and arrange between the watercress with the apple.

4 To make the horseradish dressing, whisk all the ingredients together, adding a little milk if too thick, then drizzle over the trout. Sprinkle over the chives and flowers if you have them.

CHIVE FLOWERS

Chives produce very attractive purple flowers in early summer and these are excellent to use as a garnish both for their appearance and flavour. Each floret should be pulled gently from the round flower head and sprinkled over the salad.

MELBA TOAST

To make Melba toast, toast thinly sliced bread then cut off the crusts and carefully slice in half horizontally using a sharp knife. Cut in half diagonally and place toasted side down in a warm oven for 15–20 minutes until the edges start to curl and the toast is crisp.

CHAPTER TWO

Leafy Salads

Lamb's lettuce (corn salad), rocket (arugula), purslane, chicory, endive, escarole and radiccio are just a few of the many interesting and delicious salad leaves available – eaten either on their own or in combination, they help to make a very interesting and attractive salad. Add a few herbs and a simple dressing using extra virgin olive oil and a mellow vinegar such as balsamic or sherry vinegar and you have the most simple, yet delicious salad accompaniment.

Flowers add flavour and colour to green salads; many flowers are edible, and herb flowers such as chives, thyme or marjoram are full of flavour. Nasturtiums, primroses, violas or geraniums are all easily obtainable at different times of the year and look stunning sprinkled over the top of salad leaves.

Opposite: *An enormous range of lettuces, salad greens and fresh herbs is available, and can make even a simple salad look exotic and smell deliciously aromatic.*

STEP 3

STEP 4

STEP 5

STEP 7

CAESAR SALAD

This salad is traditionally made with cos (romaine) lettuce, although any crisp variety can be used.

SERVES 4

4 tbsp olive oil
2 tbsp lemon juice
2 garlic cloves, crushed
1 tsp Worcestershire sauce
1 egg
6 quail's eggs
1 large cos (romaine) lettuce
30 g/1 oz block of Parmesan cheese
2 slices bread, crusts removed
4 tbsp corn oil
salt and pepper

1 Mix together the olive oil, lemon juice, garlic and Worcestershire sauce with salt and pepper to taste. Put the single egg in a blender or food processor and blend for 30 seconds. Add the oil mixture gradually through the feeder tube until the dressing thickens slightly.

2 If you do not have a food processor, you can make the dressing using a hand-held electric whisk, or a hand whisk. Put the egg in a small bowl and whisk in the garlic, Worcestershire sauce and seasoning. Gradually whisk in the oil and finally add the lemon juice.

3 Boil the quail's eggs for 5 minutes, then plunge into cold water to cool. Crack the shells and remove the eggs very carefully, then cut the eggs into quarters.

4 Tear the lettuce into manageable-sized pieces and put into a salad bowl with the quail's eggs.

5 Using a potato peeler, shave peelings off the Parmesan cheese.

6 Cut the bread into 5 mm/¼ inch cubes and fry in the corn oil until golden. Drain well on paper towels.

7 Pour the dressing over the salad and toss thoroughly, then sprinkle the croûtons and Parmesan shavings over the top.

STEP 1

STEP 2

STEP 4

STEP 5

SPINACH & BACON SALAD

Use only young tender spinach leaves for this recipe, as the older ones can be rather tough.

SERVES 4

250 g/8 oz young spinach leaves
1 avocado
3 tbsp French dressing (see page 8)
2 slices bread, crusts removed
3 tbsp olive oil
175 g/6 oz/5 slices thick back bacon, derinded
1 garlic clove, chopped
1 tbsp cider vinegar

1 Trim the stalks from the spinach and put the leaves into a salad bowl.

2 Halve the avocado and remove the stone (pit) by stabbing it with a sharp knife and twisting it to loosen. Peel the avocado, slice into a small bowl and toss in the French dressing until well coated. Add to the spinach and toss together.

3 Cut the bread into small triangles and fry in the olive oil until golden. Remove from the pan and drain well on paper towels.

4 Cut the bacon into strips.

5 Add the bacon to the pan and cook until it begins to brown, then add the garlic and fry for a further minute. Transfer the bacon to the salad bowl, using a perforated spoon.

6 Add the cider vinegar to the pan and stir to dissolve any juices, then pour over the salad. Sprinkle with the croûtons.

AVOCADOS

When ripe, an avocado should yield to gentle pressure at the pointed end. If you want to ripen them quickly, place them in a fruit bowl with ripe bananas. When halved, they will turn brown very quickly, so brush the cut surfaces with lemon juice.

STEP 1

STEP 2

STEP 3

STEP 4

MIXED LEAF SALAD WITH FLOWERS

A green leafy salad made from as many varieties of salad leaves and flowers as you can find.

SERVES 6

½ head frisée (chicory)
½ head feuille de chêne (oak leaf lettuce) or
  quattro stagione
few leaves of radiccio
1 head chicory (endive)
30 g/1 oz/½ cup rocket (arugula) leaves
few sprigs fresh basil or flat-leaf parsley
6 tbsp French Dressing (see page 8)
flowers of your choice (see below)

1 Tear the frisée (chicory), feuille de chêne (oak leaf lettuce) and radiccio into manageable pieces.

2 Place the salad leaves (greens) into a large serving bowl, or individual bowls if you prefer.

3 Cut the chicory (endive) into diagonal slices and add to the bowl with the rocket (arugula) leaves, basil or parsley.

4 Pour the dressing over the salad and toss thoroughly.

5 Scatter a mixture of flowers over the top.

EDIBLE FLOWERS

Violas, rock geraniums, nasturtiums, chive flowers and pot marigolds add vibrant colours and a sweet flavour to any salad, and will turn this simple salad into an unusual dish. Use it as a centrepiece at a dinner party, or to liven up a simple everyday meal.

ROCKET (ARUGULA)

The young green leaves of this plant have a distinct warm, peppery flavour and are delicious used in green salads. It is extremely easy to grow and once you have sown it in the garden or greenhouse you will always have plenty, as it re-seeds itself all over the place!

CHICORY (ENDIVE) & AVOCADO SALAD

A simple and refreshing salad to serve on hot sunny days. The contrast of the pink grapefruit, creamy chicory (endive) and bright green lamb's lettuce (corn salad) make this a stunning accompaniment.

SERVES 4

1 pink grapefruit
1 avocado
1 packet lamb's lettuce (corn salad), washed
   thoroughly
2 heads chicory (endive), sliced diagonally
1 tbsp chopped fresh mint

FRENCH DRESSING:
3 tbsp olive oil
1 tbsp wine vinegar
1 small garlic clove, crushed
$\frac{1}{2}$ tsp Dijon or Meaux mustard
1 tsp clear honey
salt and pepper

1 Peel the grapefruit with a serrated-edge knife.

2 Cut the grapefruit into segments by cutting between the membranes.

3 To make the French dressing, put all the ingredients into a screw-top jar and shake vigorously.

4 Halve the avocado and remove the stone (pit) by stabbing the stone (pit) with a sharp knife and twisting to loosen. Remove the skin.

5 Cut the avocado into small slices, put into a bowl and toss in the French dressing.

6 Remove any stalks from the lamb's lettuce (corn salad) and put into a bowl with the grapefruit, chicory (endive) and mint.

7 Add the avocado and 2 tablespoons of the French dressing. Toss well and transfer to serving plates.

LAMB'S LETTUCE (CORN SALAD)

This is so called because the shape of its dark green leaves resembles a lamb's tongue. It is also known as corn salad and the French call it *mâche*. It is easy to grow in the garden and will withstand the frost.

STEP 1

STEP 2

STEP 5

STEP 6

STEP 2

STEP 4

STEP 5

STEP 6

ROCKET (ARUGULA) & ORANGE SALAD WITH LEMON DRESSING

Pine kernels (nuts) give a delicious flavour to this salad, but be careful when browning them as they burn very easily.

SERVES 4

1 Frillice or frisée lettuce (chicory)
2 oranges
1 avocado, halved and stoned (pitted)
30 g/1 oz/¼ cup pine kernels (nuts)
30 g/1 oz/½ cup rocket (arugula) leaves

LEMON DRESSING:
finely grated rind of ½ lemon
2 tbsp lemon juice
2 tbsp olive oil
1 tsp clear honey
salt and pepper

1 Tear the lettuce into manageable pieces and place in a salad bowl.

2 Remove the pith and rind from the oranges and cut the flesh into segments. Put the flesh into the salad bowl.

3 Peel the avocado and cut into slices. Put the slices into the salad bowl.

4 Heat a heavy-based frying pan (skillet), add the pine kernels (nuts) and cook until they are golden, shaking the pan constantly.

5 Whisk all the dressing ingredients together with seasoning to taste.

6 Add the rocket (arugula) leaves to the salad bowl, pour over the dressing and toss thoroughly.

STONING (PITTING) AN AVOCADO

To stone (pit) an avocado, cut through to the stone (pit) lengthways then twist the two halves against each other to separate. Chop into the stone (pit) with a sharp knife so that it sticks in firmly then twist sharply; this will release the stone (pit), which will come away with the knife.

STEP 1

STEP 2

STEP 3

STEP 4

SALADE FRISÉE WITH NASTURTIUMS

The addition of nasturtiums make this unusual salad very appealing to the eye, and will be a talking point at any dinner party.

SERVES 4

$^1/_2$ head frisée (chicory)
250 g/8 oz packet lamb's lettuce (corn salad), washed thoroughly
2 slices bread, crusts removed
4 tbsp corn oil for frying
nasturtium flowers

FRENCH DRESSING:
3 tbsp olive oil
1 tbsp wine vinegar
1 small garlic clove, crushed
$^1/_2$ tsp Dijon or Meaux mustard
1 tsp clear honey
salt and pepper

1 Tear the frisée (chicory) into manageable pieces and put into a bowl.

2 Trim the roots of the lamb's lettuce (corn salad) and add to the bowl.

3 Cut the bread into 10 mm/$^1/_2$ inch cubes. Heat the corn oil in a frying-pan (skillet).

4 Fry the cubes of bread until golden brown. Remove from the pan and drain well on paper towels.

5 To make the French dressing, put all the ingredients in a screw-top jar and shake vigorously until blended. Pour 4 tablespoons of dressing over the salad and toss thoroughly.

6 Sprinkle the croûtons over the salad and arrange the nasturtium flowers on top.

TIPS

It is easier to cut bread into neat cubes if it is half-frozen. You can use either white or brown bread for croûtons.

For a slightly different dressing, add 1 tablespoon of chopped herbs such as chives and mint.

Nasturtium flowers have a peppery bite that enhances the flavour of any green salad. Nasturtiums are worth cultivating both for the leaves and flowers, and they are now available in many supermarkets.

CHAPTER THREE

Main Course Salads

There are plenty of ideas here for quick, colourful delicious lunches, perfect for a summer's day. Some of the recipes will give you the chance to try a warm salad, such as Warm Calf's Liver Salad and Turkish Lamb Salad, which have hot dressings poured over them just before they are served. Most can be prepared in advance, so you merely do an assembly job when you are ready to eat, allowing you to spend more time in the sun than in the kitchen.

Included here are the traditional Greek Salad, *Horiatiki*, made with tomatoes, Feta cheese and olives; and Salad Niçoise from Provence – wonderful served with your favourite wine in the shade of a leafy tree.

A basketful of ciabatta, some olive bread, an onion baguette or some Tomato Toasts (page 12) will enhance any of these salads enormously.

Opposite: *Main course salads can be made of almost anything, from the traditional salad ingredients to fruit, winter vegetables, cheese, meat, nuts, pulses and lentils.*

STEP 1

STEP 2

STEP 4

STEP 4

GREEK SALAD

A rustic, peasant salad that makes a delicious lunch on a hot, sunny day. Remember that Feta cheese is inclined to be salty, so go gently with the seasoning.

SERVES 4

¹/₂ cucumber
1 small onion, sliced thinly into rings
1 green (bell) pepper, cored, deseeded and chopped
500 g/ 1 lb tomatoes
4 tbsp olive oil
1 tbsp cider vinegar
1 tbsp chopped fresh basil
1 tbsp chopped fresh oregano
250 g/ 8 oz Feta cheese
salt and pepper
60 g/ 2 oz/ ¹/₂ cup black olives, pitted, to garnish

1 Cut the cucumber into large dice and put into a bowl with the sliced onion and chopped green (bell) pepper.

2 Cut each tomato into 8 wedges and add to the bowl with the oil, vinegar, herbs, and salt and pepper to taste.

3 Toss all the ingredients thoroughly and turn into a salad bowl.

4 Cut the Feta cheese into cubes. Sprinkle the cheese evenly over the salad.

5 Garnish with the olives and serve with plenty of crusty bread to mop up the juices.

TIP

Use Greek kalamata olives if possible. They are a purple-brown colour and have a superior flavour to other varieties.

FETA CHEESE

Feta cheese is a Greek cheese traditionally made from ewe's milk and preserved in brine. Now it is often made from cow's milk. It is a white crumbly cheese with a firm texture and is often quite salty, depending on how long it has been left in brine.

STEP 1

STEP 2

STEP 3

STEP 4

SPICED CHICKEN & GRAPE MAYONNAISE

Tender chicken breast, sweet grapes and crisp celery coated in a mild curry mayonnaise make a wonderful al fresco lunch served with spiced rice and a green salad.

SERVES 4

*500 g/1 lb cooked chicken breast
2 celery sticks
250 g/8 oz/2 cups black grapes
60 g/2 oz/¹/₂ cup split almonds,
    browned
paprika
fresh coriander (cilantro) or flat-leaf parsley
    to garnish*

*CURRY MAYONNAISE:
150 ml/¹/₄ pint/²/₃ cup mayonnaise
125 g/4 oz/¹/₂ cup natural fromage frais
1 tbsp clear honey
1 tbsp curry sauce*

1 Cut the chicken into fairly large pieces and slice the celery finely.

2 Halve the grapes, remove the seeds and place in a bowl with the chicken and celery.

3 To make the curry mayonnaise, mix all the ingredients together until blended.

4 Pour the mayonnaise over the salad and mix together carefully until well coated.

5 Transfer to a shallow serving dish and sprinkle with the almonds and paprika. Garnish with the coriander (cilantro) or parsley.

BROWNING ALMONDS

To brown almonds, place them on a baking sheet and place in a hot oven for 5–10 minutes until golden brown.

CORIANDER (CILANTRO)

Coriander (cilantro) is an intensely aromatic herb which is used extensively in Indian cookery. The seeds are ground to give a warm spicy flavour quite unlike the fresh variety. Its pretty lacy leaves make it an excellent and attractive garnish.

STEP 2

STEP 3

STEP 4

STEP 5

PASTA PROVENCAL

Use any pasta shape for this salad, but drain the pasta thoroughly so that it does not dilute the dressing. You could substitute tuna fish for the chicken to make a change.

SERVES 4

175 g/6 oz pasta
4 tbsp French Dressing (see page 8)
350 g/12 oz chicken breast
2 tbsp olive oil
2 courgettes (zucchini)
1 red (bell) pepper
2 garlic cloves
4 tomatoes
60 g/2 oz can of anchovies, drained
30 g/1 oz/¼ cup black olives
sprig of fresh parsley to garnish

1 Cook the pasta in boiling salted water for 10–12 minutes until *al dente*. Drain and rinse in hot water, then drain again thoroughly.

2 Put into a bowl with the dressing and mix together.

3 Cut the chicken breast into strips. Heat the oil in a frying pan (skillet). Add the chicken and stir-fry for 4–5 minutes, stirring occasionally until cooked, then remove from the pan.

4 Slice the courgettes (zucchini). Core and deseed the red (bell) pepper and cut into chunks. Slice the garlic, add to the pan with the courgettes (zucchini) and (bell) pepper and fry for 12–15 minutes, stirring occasionally, until softened.

5 Cut the tomatoes into wedges, chop the anchovies roughly, and halve and pit the olives. Add to the pasta with the chicken and fried vegetables, and mix together.

6 Transfer to a serving dish, garnish with parsley and serve immediately while warm.

PASTA SHAPES

For some suitable pasta shapes, choose from the following; farfalle (bow ties), conchiglie (shells), conchiglie rigate (ridged shells), penne (quill shapes), rigatoni (tubular pasta, usually ridged), fusilli (spiral shapes), rotelle (wheels) and orecchiette (little ears).

TURKISH LAMB SALAD

The bread in this salad is an unusual addition but it soaks up the dressing well and has a delicious flavour. The charred meat and creamy yogurt complete a delightful salad for a light lunch.

STEP 2

SERVES 4

2 red (bell) peppers, cored, and deseeded
1 yellow (bell) pepper, cored and deseeded
1 green (bell) pepper, cored and deseeded
4 tomatoes, skinned
1 small onion
500 g/1 lb lamb fillet (tenderloin)
3 pitta breads
4 tbsp Tomato Vinaigrette (see page 10)
120 ml/4 fl oz/¹/₂ cup thick, creamy yogurt
3 tbsp chopped fresh parsley

1 To skin the (bell) peppers, lay them cut-side down on a grill (broiler) pan and cook gently until blackened. Put in a plastic bag to cool.

2 Remove the (bell) pepper skin and chop roughly. Cut each tomato into 8 wedges and slice the onion. Put the onion into a bowl with the tomato wedges and (bell) pepper chunks.

3 Place the lamb fillet (tenderloin) under a preheated medium-hot grill (broiler) until charred on the outside but still pink in the middle.

4 Cut the bread into pieces and add to the bowl with the (bell) peppers, onion and tomato. Pour over the

dressing, mix together thoroughly and arrange on individual plates.

5 Slice the lamb and arrange a few pieces over each salad. Drizzle over the yogurt and sprinkle with the parsley.

STEP 3

STEP 4

VARIATION

You may prefer to use a half leg of lamb instead of lamb fillet (tenderloin). If so, cut it into cubes, thread the meat on to skewers and cook for 3–4 minutes on each side under a hot grill (broiler). Then slide off the skewers and arrange over the salad.

STEP 5

STEP 2

STEP 4

STEP 5

STEP 6

WARM CALF'S LIVER SALAD

The delicate flavour of calf's liver is enhanced with a dressing of balsamic vinegar and fresh sage. The liver should be cooked very briefly so that it is still pink inside. Chicken livers can be used instead of calf's liver, if you prefer.

SERVES 2

250 g/8 oz packet of mixed salad leaves
    (greens)
250 g/8 oz calf's liver
1 orange, cut into segments
2 tbsp pine kernels (nuts)
3 tbsp olive oil
1 garlic clove, sliced
2 tsp chopped sage
2 tbsp balsamic vinegar
salt and pepper

1 Arrange the salad leaves (greens) on 2 individual plates. Cut the liver into large pieces.

2 Peel the orange using a serrated knife, then divide into segments.

3 Put the pine kernels (nuts) in a small heavy-based frying pan (skillet) and cook over a moderate heat, shaking the pan constantly so that the nuts do not burn. Remove the nuts from the pan.

4 Heat the oil in a heavy-based frying pan (skillet). Add the liver to the pan with the garlic and sage, and fry for 1–2 minutes, depending on the thickness of the liver, turning it once.

5 Remove the liver, using a perforated spoon, and arrange on the salad with the orange segments.

6 Add the vinegar to the frying pan (skillet) with any juices from the orange and stir well to deglaze the pan. Season to taste.

7 Sprinkle the pine kernels (nuts) over the salads, then pour over the juices and serve immediately.

CALF'S LIVER

Calf's liver is generally considered to be the finest in quality and flavour, but is also the most expensive. It should be thinly sliced and fried briefly so that it is still pink inside.

SALADE NICOISE

An ideal salad for a summer lunch. It is particularly delicious served with hot garlic bread.

STEP 2

STEP 3

STEP 4

STEP 6

SERVES 4

1 small crisp lettuce
500 g/ 1 lb tomatoes
200 g/ 7 oz can of tuna fish, drained
2 tbsp chopped fresh parsley
½ cucumber
1 small red onion, sliced
250 g/ 8 oz French (green) beans, topped
   and tailed, cooked
1 small red (bell) pepper, cored and deseeded
6 tbsp French Dressing (see page 8)
3 hard-boiled (hard-cooked) eggs
60 g/ 2 oz can of anchovies, drained
12 black olives, pitted

1 Place the lettuce leaves in a mixing bowl.

2 Cut the tomatoes into wedges, flake the tuna fish and put both into the bowl with the parsley.

3 Cut the cucumber in half lengthways, then cut into slices. Slice the onion. Add the cucumber and onion to the bowl.

4 Cut the French (green) beans in half, chop the red (bell) pepper and add both to the bowl.

5 Pour over the French dressing and toss thoroughly, then spoon into a salad bowl to serve.

6 Cut the eggs into quarters, arrange over the top with the anchovies and scatter with the olives.

GARLIC BREAD

To make garlic bread, cream 90 g/3 oz/ ⅓ cup butter with 2 crushed garlic cloves and seasoning to taste. Slice a French stick diagonally without cutting right through, so the pieces stay attached. Spread both sides of each slice with the garlic butter. Wrap in foil and put in a hot oven for about 10 minutes. Unwrap and leave in the oven to crisp for 5 minutes.

CHAPTER FOUR

Substantial Salads

Many of these salads are delicious served warm and can be
prepared quickly just before you eat. Comforting warm lentils with
frankfurters are enlivened with an olive and tomato dressing.
Warm pasta tossed in a fresh basil vinaigrette tastes wonderful.
Beans too make a delicious salad, as many varieties as you like –
the more the merrier when it comes to a mixture of colours and
flavours. Enhance them with a dressing of soy sauce and garlic, and
for that extra zip, add a bouquet of chopped coriander (cilantro).

There are salads here to satisfy every taste and appetite, from the
gourmet to the ravenous, from the delicate flavour of wild rice with
mint and mango to a hugely satisfying hot potato salad in a
garlicky dressing of olives and tomato.

*Opposite: The addition of filling
ingredients such as potatoes and
root vegetables to the usual
range of salad ingredients turns
any salad into a satisfying meal.*

STEP 2

STEP 3

STEP 4

STEP 5

WARM PASTA WITH BASIL VINAIGRETTE

All the ingredients of pesto sauce are included here – basil, pine kernels (nuts), Parmesan cheese and olive oil. Sun-dried tomatoes and olives complete this delicious salad, which is just as tasty served cold.

SERVES 4

250 g/8 oz pasta spirals
4 tomatoes
60 g/2 oz/¹⁄₂ cup black olives
30 g/1 oz/¹⁄₄ cup sun-dried tomatoes
2 tbsp pine kernels (nuts), browned
2 tbsp Parmesan cheese shavings
sprig of fresh basil to garnish

BASIL VINAIGRETTE:
4 tbsp chopped fresh basil
1 garlic clove, crushed
2 tbsp grated Parmesan cheese
4 tbsp olive oil
2 tbsp lemon juice
pepper

1 Cook the pasta in boiling salted water for 10–12 minutes until *al dente*. Drain and rinse well in hot water, then drain again thoroughly.

2 To make the vinaigrette, mix the basil, garlic, Parmesan cheese, olive oil, lemon juice and pepper together with a whisk until blended.

3 Put the pasta into a bowl, pour over the basil vinaigrette and toss thoroughly.

4 Skin the tomatoes and cut into wedges. Halve and pit the olives and slice the sun-dried tomatoes.

5 Add them all to the pasta and mix together thoroughly. Transfer to a salad bowl and scatter the nuts and Parmesan shavings over the top. Serve warm, garnished with a sprig of basil.

SUN-DRIED TOMATOES

Sun-dried tomatoes are, as their name indicates, tomatoes that have been halved and dried in the sun, leaving a wrinkled specimen with an extremely rich, concentrated flavour. They are usually covered with oil, and herbs and garlic are added to give extra flavour. When added to a sauce or salad they impart an added depth of flavour, and are also delicious eaten straight from the jar with a chunk of fresh bread.

STEP 1

STEP 2

STEP 3

STEP 5

LENTIL & FRANKFURTER SALAD

The tiny brown-green lentils from Puy in France are the finest – they have a really distinctive flavour. The larger green or brown lentils are also good and ideal in salads as they retain their shape when cooked.

SERVES 8

250 g/8 oz/1 cup green lentils
4 tbsp sunflower oil
1 tbsp soy sauce
1 tbsp wine vinegar
1 garlic clove, crushed
4 frankfurters
1 onion
1 red (bell) pepper
2 celery sticks
4 tomatoes
2 tbsp chopped fresh parsley
1 tbsp chopped fresh marjoram
salt and pepper

1 Put the lentils into a pan of boiling salted water, bring back to the boil and cook for 35–40 minutes until softened. Drain well and put into a bowl.

2 Add the oil, soy sauce, vinegar and garlic with seasoning to taste, and mix with the lentils while still warm. Leave to cool.

3 Cut the frankfurters into diagonal slices and chop the onion finely.

4 Core and deseed the (bell) pepper and chop roughly.

5 Cut the celery into thin diagonal slices.

6 Skin the tomatoes and cut into slices, then add to the lentils with the frankfurters, onion, (bell) pepper, celery and herbs. Mix together well and transfer to a serving dish.

VARIATION

Instead of frankfurters, you could use cubes of smoked ham or chopped fried bacon.

STEP 2

STEP 3

STEP 4

STEP 5

MANGO & WILD RICE SALAD

Technically, wild rice is not rice at all but comes from a wild aquatic grass native to North America. It has a nutty flavour and is slightly chewy. Add the dressing while the rice is still hot; this way it absorbs the flavour better.

SERVES 4

60 g/2 oz/^{1}/$_3$ cup wild rice
60 g/2 oz/^{1}/$_3$ cup basmati rice
3 tbsp hazelnut oil
1 tbsp sherry vinegar
1 small mango
2 celery sticks
60 g/2 oz/^{1}/$_2$ cup ready-to-eat dried apricots, chopped
60 g/2 oz/^{1}/$_2$ cup split almonds, browned
2 tbsp chopped fresh mint
salt and pepper

1 Cook the rice in separate saucepans in boiling salted water – the wild rice for 45–50 minutes, the basmati for 10–12 minutes. Drain, rinse well and drain again thoroughly.

2 Mix the oil, vinegar and seasoning together and pour over the rice in a bowl.

3 Cut the mango in half lengthways as close to the stone (pit) as possible. Remove the stone (pit), using a sharp knife.

4 Peel off the skin and cut the flesh into slices.

5 Slice the celery finely and add to the cooled rice with the apricots, mango, browned almonds and chopped mint. Mix together thoroughly and transfer to a serving bowl.

BROWNING ALMONDS

To brown almonds, place on a baking sheet in a moderate oven for 5–10 minutes until golden brown. Alternatively, they can be browned under a moderate grill (broiler), turning frequently, as they burn quickly. Cool before adding to the salad so that they are crisp.

POTATOES IN OLIVE & TOMATO DRESSING

The warm potatoes quickly absorb the wonderful flavours of olives, tomatoes and olive oil. I love this salad when served warm, but it is also good served cold.

STEP 2

SERVES 4

750 g/ 1½ lb waxy potatoes
1 shallot
2 tomatoes
1 tbsp chopped fresh basil
salt

TOMATO AND OLIVE DRESSING:
1 tomato, skinned and chopped finely
4 black olives, pitted and chopped finely
4 tbsp olive oil
1 tbsp wine vinegar
1 garlic clove, crushed
salt and pepper

1 Cook the potatoes in boiling salted water for 15 minutes until they are tender.

2 Drain the potatoes well, chop roughly and put into a bowl.

3 Chop the shallot. Cut the tomatoes into wedges and add the shallot and tomatoes to the potatoes.

4 To make the dressing, put all the ingredients into a screw-top jar and mix together thoroughly.

5 Pour the dressing over the potato mixture and toss thoroughly.

6 Transfer the salad to a serving dish and sprinkle with the chopped fresh basil.

STEP 3

STEP 4

TIPS

I often make this with floury (mealy) potatoes. It doesn't look so attractive, as the potatoes break up when they are cooked, but they absorb the dressing wonderfully.

Be sure to use an extra virgin olive oil for the dressing to give a really fruity flavour to the potatoes.

STEP 5

BEAN SALAD WITH SOY DRESSING

Any canned beans can be used in this salad; there are a wide variety available. To make a light lunch, I add a spicy garlic sausage or some flaked tuna fish.

STEP 1

STEP 2

STEP 4

SERVES 8

400 g/13 oz can of flageolet (small navy)
 beans, drained
400 g/13 oz can of red kidney beans,
 drained
400 g/13 oz can of pinto beans, drained
1/2 red onion, sliced finely
175 g/6 oz French (green) beans, topped
 and tailed
1 red (bell) pepper
2 tbsp chopped fresh coriander (cilantro)
sprig of fresh coriander (cilantro) to garnish

SOY DRESSING:
1 cm/1/2 inch piece ginger root
1 garlic clove
3 tbsp olive oil
2 tsp red wine vinegar
1/2 tbsp soy sauce
1 tsp chilli sauce
1 tsp sesame oil

1 Put the flageolet (small navy), red kidney and pinto beans into a bowl. Add the sliced onion to the beans.

2 Cut the French (green) beans into 2.5 cm/1 inch lengths and cook in boiling salted water for 10 minutes until just tender. Drain thoroughly and add to the bowl.

3 Lay the red (bell) pepper cut-side down on a grill (broiler) pan and cook gently until blackened. Put in a plastic bag to cool. Remove the skin and chop roughly.

4 To make the dressing, chop the ginger root finely, crush the garlic and place in a screw-top jar with the olive oil, vinegar, soy sauce, chilli sauce and sesame oil. Shake vigorously.

5 Add the dressing to the salad with the red (bell) pepper and coriander (cilantro) and mix together thoroughly. Transfer to a serving dish and garnish with a sprig of coriander (cilantro).

VARIATION

For a change, you could use chick peas (garbanzo beans) instead of one of the cans of beans. Frozen broad (fava) beans or peas also make pleasant alternatives.

STEP 5

STEP 1

STEP 2

STEP 4

STEP 5

WARM BULGAR & CORIANDER (CILANTRO) SALAD

Bulgar wheat is ready to eat after soaking and needs no further cooking. Coriander (cilantro) has a pungent smell that you either love or hate. It gives this salad an exciting bite.

SERVES 4

175 g/6 oz/1½ cups bulgar wheat
1 onion
1 garlic clove
1 red (bell) pepper
3 tbsp olive oil
2 tsp ground cumin
2 tsp ground coriander
2 tomatoes
2 tbsp lemon juice
4 tbsp currants
2 tbsp chopped fresh coriander (cilantro)
4 tbsp pine kernels (nuts), browned

1 Soak the bulgar wheat in salted boiling water for 20 minutes. Chop the onion and garlic, and core, deseed and chop the red (bell) pepper.

2 Heat the oil in a pan and fry the onion, garlic and (bell) pepper for about 5 minutes until softened.

3 Add the spices and cook for a further 1 minute.

4 Drain the bulgar through a sieve (strainer), pressing out as much liquid as possible.

5 Chop the tomatoes, then add to the pan with the bulgar, lemon juice and currants and mix together thoroughly.

6 Transfer to a serving dish and sprinkle with the coriander (cilantro) and pine kernels (nuts). Serve while warm.

HELPFUL HINTS

Cous-cous can be used instead of bulgar wheat for this salad, and is prepared in a similar manner. Cous-cous is semolina grains that have been dampened and rolled in flour. Bulgar wheat is cracked wheat that has been partially cooked.

STEP 2

STEP 4

STEP 5

STEP 6

POTATO & SMOKED HAM MAYONNAISE

A delicious mixture of potato, egg and smoked ham mixed with a mustard mayonnaise, ideal for a light lunch. You can use sliced frankfurters cut into cubes instead of the smoked ham if you prefer.

SERVES 4

750 g/1¹/₂ lb new potatoes, scrubbed
4 spring onions (scallions), chopped
2 tbsp French Dressing (see page 8)
150 ml/¹/₄ pint/²/₃ cup mayonnaise
3 tbsp thick natural yogurt
1 tbsp Dijon mustard
2 eggs
250 g/8 oz slice of smoked ham
3 dill pickles
2 tbsp chopped fresh dill

1 Cook the potatoes in boiling salted water for 15 minutes until just tender, then drain.

2 Cut into pieces and put into a bowl while still warm with the spring onion (scallion) and dressing and mix together.

3 Mix the mayonnaise, yogurt and mustard together.

4 Boil the eggs for 12 minutes, then plunge into cold water to cool. Shell and chop roughly.

5 Cut the smoked ham into cubes and slice the dill pickles.

6 Add to the potatoes with the egg. Pour over the mayonnaise and mix together thoroughly, but carefully.

7 Transfer to a serving dish and sprinkle with the dill.

DILL

Dill is a very popular herb in Scandinavia, central Europe and Russia. It is particularly good with cucumber, beetroot, fish and potato dishes. It has very pretty delicate, feathery fronds which makes it an excellent garnish too. Fennel would be a good substitute, but has a stronger, more aniseedy flavour.

CHAPTER FIVE

Fruit Salads

Italy, Scandinavia and the Caribbean have all been raided to offer up their fruitful treasures. From the Caribbean there are the delights of paw-paw (papaya), mango, guava and my own favourite, passion-fruit. From Italy, sun-ripened figs and succulent peaches are made ever more indulgent by pouring over a liqueur-flavoured cream and sugar, and then grilling them until the topping has caramelized. For the more calorie-conscious, try the Tropical Salad, a mixture of fruits from the Caribbean soaked in Jamaican rum, or Summer Fruit Salad – a mixture of soft red fruits in a sauce of orange and port wine.

If you need any addition to these exotic salads, try natural fromage frais, or a thick, creamy, natural yogurt, either as they are or with a dash of liqueur stirred in. In most of the recipes the fruits are interchangeable according to the season, so do experiment to find your favourite combination.

Opposite: The vibrant colours of fresh fruit ensure an appealing and striking dessert.

STEP 2

STEP 4

STEP 5

STEP 6

SUMMER FRUIT SALAD

A mixture of soft summer fruits in an orange-flavoured syrup with a dash of port. Serve with fromage frais or whipped cream.

SERVES 6

90 g/3 oz/¹/₃ cup caster (superfine) sugar
75 ml/3 fl oz/¹/₃ cup water
grated rind and juice of 1 small orange
250 g/8 oz/2 cups redcurrants, stripped
 from their stalks
2 tsp arrowroot
2 tbsp port
125 g/4 oz/1 cup blackberries
125 g/4 oz/1 cup blueberries
125 g/4 oz/³/₄ cup strawberries
250 g/8 oz/1¹/₂ cups raspberries

1 Put the sugar, water and grated orange rind into a pan and heat gently, stirring until the sugar has dissolved.

2 Add the redcurrants and orange juice, bring to the boil and simmer gently for 2–3 minutes.

3 Strain the fruit, reserving the syrup, and put into a bowl.

4 Blend the arrowroot with a little water. Return the syrup to the pan, add the arrowroot and bring to the boil, stirring until thickened.

5 Add the port and mix together well. Then pour over the redcurrants in the bowl.

6 Add the blackberries, blueberries, strawberries and raspberries. Mix together and leave to cool.

7 Serve in individual glass dishes with natural fromage frais or cream.

USING FROZEN FRUIT

Although this salad is really best made with fresh fruits in season, you can achieve an acceptable result with frozen equivalents, with perhaps the exception of strawberries. You can buy frozen fruits of the forest in most supermarkets, which would be ideal.

STEP 1

STEP 2

STEP 3

STEP 5

MELON & KIWI SALAD

A refreshing fruit salad, ideal to serve after a rich meal. Charentais or cantaloupe melons are also good. Physalis (ground cherries), also known as Cape gooseberries, make a delightful decoration. Peel back the thin papery husks to expose the golden berries.

SERVES 6

½ Galia melon
2 kiwi fruit
125 g/4 oz/1 cup white (green) seedless
    grapes
1 paw-paw (papaya), halved
3 tbsp orange-flavoured liqueur such as
    Cointreau
1 tbsp chopped lemon verbena, lemon balm
    or mint
sprigs of lemon verbena or physalis (ground
    cherries) to decorate

1 Remove the seeds from the melon, cut into 4 slices and cut away the skin. Cut the flesh into cubes and put into a bowl.

2 Peel the kiwi fruit and cut across into slices. Add to the melon with the grapes.

3 Remove the seeds from the paw-paw (papaya) and cut off the skin. Slice the flesh thickly and cut into diagonal pieces.

4 Mix together the liqueur and lemon verbena, pour over the fruit and leave for 1 hour, stirring it occasionally.

5 Spoon into glasses, pour over the juices and decorate with lemon verbena sprigs or physalis (ground cherries).

LEMON BALM

Lemon balm or sweet balm is a fragrant lemon-scented plant with slightly hairy serrated leaves and a pronounced lemon flavour. Lemon verbena can also be used – this has an even stronger lemon flavour and smooth elongated leaves. Both can be used as a herbal infusion, which is soothing, refreshing and delicious.

STEP 2

STEP 3

STEP 4

STEP 5

MANGO & PASSION-FRUIT SALAD WITH MASCARPONE CREAM

An exotic salad of mango, oranges and passion-fruit soaked in liqueur and served with a rich silken cream. Passion-fruit are ready to eat when their skins are well dimpled.

SERVES 4

1 large mango
2 oranges
4 passion-fruit
2 tbsp orange-flavoured liqueur such as
    Grand Marnier
mint or geranium leaves to decorate

MASCARPONE CREAM
125 g/4 oz/½ cup Mascarpone cheese
1 tbsp clear honey
4 tbsp thick, natural yogurt
few drops of vanilla flavouring (extract)

1 Cut the mango in half lengthwise as close to the stone (pit) as possible. Remove the stone (pit), using a sharp knife.

2 Peel off the skin, cut the flesh into slices and put into a bowl.

3 Peel the oranges, removing all the pith, and cut into segments. Add to the bowl with any juices.

4 Halve the passion-fruit, scoop out the flesh and add to the bowl with the liqueur. Mix well and chill for 1 hour. Turn into glass dishes.

5 To make the Mascarpone cream, blend the Mascarpone cheese and honey together. Stir in the yogurt and vanilla flavouring (extract) until thoroughly blended.

6 Serve the fruit salad with the Mascarpone cream, decorated with mint or geranium leaves.

MASCARPONE

Mascarpone is a deliciously rich, soft cream cheese from Italy. It has a smooth silky texture with the flavour of cream. As it has a close texture, I usually add a liqueur or some yogurt to give it a softer consistency.

TROPICAL SALAD

Paw-paws (papayas) are ready to eat when they yield to gentle pressure applied in the palm of your hand. Use baby pineapples if you can, as the salad looks even more stunning served in the shells.

STEP 1

STEP 3

STEP 4

STEP 5

SERVES 8

1 paw-paw (papaya)
2 tbsp fresh orange juice
3 tbsp rum
2 bananas
2 guavas
1 small pineapple or 2 baby pineapples
2 passion-fruit, halved
pineapple leaves to decorate

1 Cut the paw-paw (papaya) in half and remove the seeds. Peel and slice the flesh into a bowl.

2 Pour over the orange juice together with the rum.

3 Slice the bananas, peel and slice the guavas, and add both to the bowl.

4 Cut the top and base from the pineapple, then cut off the skin.

5 Slice the pineapple flesh, discard the core, cut into pieces and add to the bowl.

6 Halve the passion-fruit, scoop out the flesh with a teaspoon, add to the bowl and stir well to mix.

7 Spoon the salad into glass bowls and decorate with pineapple leaves.

PINEAPPLES

If you are using baby pineapples, cut them in half lengthways and scoop out the flesh after loosening with a grapefruit knife. Cut the flesh into pieces and use the shells to serve the salad in.

GUAVAS

Guavas come from the Caribbean, Thailand and Central America. They have a heavenly smell when ripe – their scent will fill a whole room. They should give to gentle pressure when ripe, and their skins should be yellow. If you cannot buy them fresh, the canned ones are very good and have a pink tinge to the flesh.

STEP 1

STEP 2

STEP 3

STEP 4

NECTARINES IN ALMOND LIQUEUR CREAM

Nectarines, figs and strawberries are grilled (broiled) with a rich liqueur-flavoured cream to give a crusted sugary finish.

SERVES 4

2 nectarines or peaches
175 g/6 oz/1½ cups strawberries
2 figs
150 ml/¼ pint/⅔ cup double (heavy)
   cream
2 tbsp almond-flavoured liqueur such as
   Amaretto di Saronno
3 tbsp demerara (brown crystal) sugar

1 Halve and stone (pit) the nectarines, then slice.

2 Hull and halve the strawberries, cut each fig into 8 wedges and arrange on 4 flameproof plates with the strawberries and nectarines.

3 Whip the cream and liqueur together until the cream just holds its shape. Spoon over the fruit on each plate.

4 Sprinkle the sugar generously over the cream.

5 Place each plate under a preheated hot grill (broiler) until bubbling and golden. Serve immediately.

TIPS

Bananas make a good alternative if you cannot get figs. Slice them into thick, diagonal slices and toss them in lemon juice to prevent them from browning.

To make the grilling (broiling) easier, you can arrange the fruit on one large platter and cover it with the liqueur-flavoured cream and sugar. This means that you will only have to grill (broil) once, and no one is left waiting for their dessert. Each person can then serve themselves from the central plate.

Make sure the sugar becomes a dark brown, almost burned, as this crispness adds a great texture and flavour to the fruit.

THE PERFECT SALAD

SALAD INGREDIENTS

Make sure you always use the freshest ingredients to ensure a successful salad. Try to ensure that you buy fruit and vegetables at their peak and use them within a few days of buying.

Every salad can be turned into something special with the addition of a few carefully chosen herbs to add flavour and a delicious aroma. For an extra special salad, add a few edible flowers, which look colourful and attractive, especially when mixed with a variety of salad leaves (greens).

Herbs

Herbs, which used to be so integral a part of English cookery, are now being rediscovered. Their use in any form of cooking is to be recommended, but in salads the addition of their fresh, aromatic leaves is of special value.

Do not be afraid to experiment. There are so many herbs from which to choose, such a variety of flavours, aromas and even colours that you can ring the changes constantly.

The flowers of herbs such as thyme, rosemary and chives can also be used to add colour and flavour.

Flowers

The fascination of flowers as an attractive garnish for salads was discovered by our

SALADS

Salads are such a versatile way of eating, and the variety of ingredients is so great, that they can be made to suit any occasion, from the light piquant starter designed to stimulate the taste buds to the more substantial dish served as a main course or the mixture of exotic fruits that makes a delicious dessert.

Salads can be fruity, fishy, meaty, eggy, cheesy or just fresh green. All are highly nutritious providing valuable minerals, vitamins and the necessary fibre. They are also generally low in calories, provided you go easy on the dressing, or use a fat-free dressing. It is easy to make a salad look attractive and appetizing, which will encourage your family to eat the fruits and vegetables which are so vital to their good health. It is also often a welcome dish to serve alongside richer offerings at a dinner party or celebration meal.

It is both worthwhile and interesting to take note of the various vegetables and fruits available in the shops at different seasons of the year. It is obviously best to use them when they are at their peak, and of course, when they are in season, as they will be plentiful and cheap. A bonus for the budget!

Supermarkets now stock many unusual ingredients, which can add interest to an ordinary salad. Experiment with new fruits and vegetables, buying them in small quantities to lend unusual flavours to salads made mostly from cheaper ingredients.

You will see from the recipes that I have been liberal in the use of herbs, which must be fresh. They add a unique 'zip' and it can be great fun trying them out to discover which are your favourites. Experiment each time you make a salad or a dressing; try marjoram, thyme, chives, basil, mint, fennel and dill as well as the ubiquitous parsley. Basil goes especially well with tomatoes, and fennel or dill are particularly good with cucumber, beetroot and fish salads.

A salad is the ideal emergency meal. It is quick to 'rustle up' and there are times when you might discover that you already have a really good combination of ingredients to hand when you need to present a meal-in-a-moment. A rapid check in the pantry might produce a can of beans or artichoke hearts. Add the couple of tomatoes and yellow (bell) pepper languishing in the salad drawer of the refrigerator, throw in a few sprigs of mint or basil that you have growing on the window sill, a few olives from that jar in the corner, a splash of dressing and you have a culinary inspiration, a super salad that you had no idea was lurking in your kitchen.

DRESSINGS

All salads depend on being well dressed and so it is necessary to use the best ingredients, and the choice of oil is particularly important.

The principal ingredients in a salad dressing are oil and vinegar with a

76

variety of other flavourings that can be varied to suit the particular ingredients in the salad.

Salad oils

Oils are produced from various nuts, seeds and beans and each has its own particular flavour. Unrefined oils have a superior taste and, although more expensive, they are definitely worth using for salad dressings.

Olive oil is the best oil for most salad dressings as its flavour is far superior to others. Choose a green-tinged, fruity oil which will be labelled 'extra virgin' or 'first pressing'.

Sesame oil has a strong nutty tang which gives an unusual flavour to dressings and is particularly good with oriental-type salads.

Sunflower and safflower oil are neutral-flavoured oils and can be mixed with olive oil or used alone to produce a lighter dressing. Mayonnaise made with a combination of one of these oils and olive oil has a lighter consistency.

Walnut and hazelnut oils have the most wonderful flavour and aroma, and are usually mixed with olive oil in a French dressing. It is especially good with slightly bitter salad plants such as chicory (endive), radiccio or spinach.

Vinegars

Vinegars such as wine, cider, sherry or herb-flavoured are essential for a good dressing. Malt vinegar is far too harsh and overpowers the subtle balance of the dressing. Lemon juice may be used if you prefer and is often preferable if the salad is fruit-based.

Cider vinegar is reputed to contain many healthy properties and valuable nutrients. It also has a light subtle flavour.

Wine vinegar is the one most commonly used for French dressing; either red or white will do.

Sherry vinegar has a rich mellow flavour which blends particularly well with walnut and hazelnut oils.

Flavoured vinegars can be made from cider and wine vinegar. To do this, steep your chosen ingredient in a small bottle of vinegar for anything up to 2 weeks. Particularly good additions are basil, tarragon, garlic, thyme, mint or rosemary. Raspberry wine vinegar can be made by adding about 12 raspberries to a bottle of vinegar.

Balsamic vinegar is dark and mellow with a sweet/sour flavour. It is expensive but you need only a few drops or at most a teaspoonful to give a wonderful taste. It is made in the area around Modena in Italy and some, made by traditional methods, are aged for many years in oak barrels.

Mustards

Mustards are made from black, brown or white mustard seeds which are ground, mixed with spices and then, usually, mixed with vinegar.

There are many flavoured mustards available, including horseradish, honey, chilli and tarragon.

Meaux mustard is made from mixed mustard seeds and has a grainy texture with a warm spicy taste.

Dijon mustard, made from husked and ground mustard seeds, is a medium hot

ancestors long ago. Apart from the delightful flavour of many, the colour contrast they provide is their main asset. Common sense is the best guide to which flowers may be used whole and which should have the petals gently separated from the calyx.

It is, of course, important that the flowers should look fresh and clean, so should they need to be washed, handle with great care and pat dry with paper towels. Store them in a sealed polythene bag in the refrigerator until required. Sprinkle them over the top of the salad just before serving so that they do not become marked by the dressing.

Borage, primroses, violas, pot marigolds, nasturtiums, violets, rock geraniums and rose petals are all suitable and impart a sweetness and intense colour contrast to any green salad. Chive flowers have a good strong flavour. They have pretty, round, mauve flower heads which should be separated into florets before sprinkling over the salad.

SALAD DRESSINGS
Make up a large bottle of your
favourite dressing and keep it
in the refrigerator until
required.

Sesame Dressing
A piquant dressing with a rich
creamy texture. Good with
beans and any oriental type
salad.

2 tbsp sesame paste (tahini)
2 tbsp cider vinegar
2 tbsp medium sherry
2 tbsp sesame oil
1 tbsp soy sauce
1 garlic clove, crushed

Put the sesame paste in a bowl
and gradually mix in the
vinegar and sherry until
smooth. Add the remaining
ingredients and mix together
thoroughly.

Tomato Dressing
A completely fat-free dressing,
ideal for the calorie and fat-
conscious.

120 ml/4 fl oz/^{1}/$_2$ cup tomato
   juice
1 garlic clove, crushed
2 tbsp lemon juice
1 tbsp soy sauce
1 tsp clear honey
2 tbsp chopped chives
salt and pepper

Put all the ingredients into a
screw-top jar and shake
vigorously.

mustard with a sharp flavour and is the
most versatile in salads. It is made in
Dijon, France, and only mustard made
there can be labelled as such.

German mustard is a mild sweet/sour
tasting mustard and is best used in
Scandinavian and German salads.

SALAD LEAVES (GREENS)
Round or cabbage lettuce is the one most
familiar to us all. I try to avoid the
hothouse variety as the leaves are limp
and floppy. There are a number of
interesting salad leaves (greens) now
available, and it is worth experimenting
to find your favourite. Some of them have
a surprisingly strong and distinctive
flavour, unlike the ordinary lettuce that
most of us are used to.

Chicory (endive)
This is available from autumn (fall) to
spring and with its slightly bitter flavour
makes an interesting addition to winter
salads. Choose firm, tightly packed cones
with yellow leaf tips. Avoid any with
damaged leaves or leaf tips that are
turning green as they will be rather too
bitter. Red chicory (endive) is also
available, mostly imported from Holland.

Chinese leaves
These are a most useful salad ingredient
available in the the autumn (fall) and
winter months. I like to shred them fairly
finely and use them as a base, adding
bean shoots and leaves such as
watercress or dandelion.

Cos (romaine) lettuce
This is a superb crisp variety used

especially in Caesar salad. It has long,
narrow, bright green leaves.

Endive (chicory)
A slightly bitter tasting but most
attractive curly-leaved salad plant. There
are two varieties; the curly endive (frisée)
which has a mop head of light green frilly
leaves and the Batavia endive (escarole)
which has broader, smoother leaves.
Before they mature, both varieties have
their leaves tied together to blanch the
centres, which produces light-coloured
tender leaves.

Feuille de chêne (oak leaf)
This red-tinged, delicately flavoured
lettuce is good when mixed with other
leaves.

Iceberg lettuce
This has pale green, densely packed
leaves. It may appear expensive, but is
extremely good value when compared
with other lettuces by weight. It has a
fresh crisp texture and keeps well in the
refrigerator, wrapped in a polythene bag

Lamb's lettuce (corn salad)
This is so called because its dark green
leaves resemble a lamb's tongue. It is also
known as corn salad and the French call
it *mâche*. It is easy to grow in the garden
and will withstand the frost. It is well
worth looking out for when it is in
season.

Purslane
This has fleshy stalks and rosettes of
succulent green leaves which have a
sharp, clean flavour. It is an excellent

addition to green salads and is widely used in France and the Middle East.

Radiccio

This is a variety of chicory (endive) originating in Italy. It looks rather like a small tightly packed red lettuce and is widely available. It is quite expensive but comparatively few leaves are needed, as it has quite a bitter flavour. The leaves are a deep purple with a white contrasting rib and add character to any green salad.

Rocket (arugula, Roquette)

The young green leaves of this plant have a distinctive warm peppery flavour and are delicious in green salads.

Watercress

This has a fresh peppery taste that recommends it to many salads. It is available throughout the year, though it is less good when flowering, or early in the season when the leaves are very small.

Preparation of salad leaves (greens)

Whichever salad leaves (greens) you choose, they should be firm and crisp with no sign of browning or wilting. Their preparation for the salad should be undertaken with care, remembering that most salad greens bruise very easily.

To prepare, pull off and discard all damaged outer leaves and wash the remaining leaves in cold salted water which will remove any insects or slugs. Dry them thoroughly, as any water left on the leaves will dilute the dressing. This can be done either by patting the leaves dry with paper towels, spinning them in a salad spinner, or by placing them in a clean tea towel (dish cloth), gathering up the loose ends and swinging the tea towel (dish cloth) around vigorously. This is best done outside, as some of the water will leak through the towel (cloth).

If the salad is not required immediately, it can be stored in a polythene bag in the salad drawer of a refrigerator.

Dressing the salad too early will cause the salad leaves (greens) to wilt. Ideally, salad leaves (greens) should be torn into manageable-sized pieces and tossed with the dressing in a large bowl just before serving.

NUTS

In addition to colour and flavour, salads need texture, which can be achieved by combining crunchy ingredients with softer fruits and vegetables, and using pasta, potatoes and lentils to contrast with such salad ingredients as (bell) peppers, celery, apples and so on. Nuts are particularly useful for adding texture to a salad, contributing a pleasant crunchiness as well as flavour, and they add to the nutritious content of the salad too, being rich in vitamins and oils.

Many nuts taste even better if they are browned before use. These include almonds, hazelnuts, pine kernels (nuts) and peanuts. To brown nuts, put them on a baking sheet and place in a hot oven for 5–10 minutes until golden brown. Pine kernels (nuts) may also be browned by placing in a dry heavy-based frying pan (skillet) and shaking over a high heat until golden brown.

Apple & Cider Vinegar Dressing
2 tbsp sunflower oil
2 tbsp concentrated apple juice
2 tbsp cider vinegar
1 tbsp Meaux mustard
1 garlic clove, crushed
salt and pepper

Put all the ingredients together in a screw-top jar and shake vigorously.

Green Herb Dressing
A pretty pale green dressing with a fresh spring-like flavour, ideal with cauliflower, broccoli or broad (fava) beans.

15 g/$\frac{1}{2}$ oz/$\frac{1}{4}$ cup fresh parsley
15 g/$\frac{1}{2}$ oz/$\frac{1}{4}$ cup mint
15 g/$\frac{1}{2}$ oz/$\frac{1}{4}$ cup chives
1 garlic clove, crushed
150 ml/$\frac{1}{4}$ pint/$\frac{2}{3}$ cup natural yogurt
salt and pepper

Remove the stalks from the parsley and mint and put the leaves in a blender or food processor with the garlic and yogurt. Add seasoning to taste. Blend until smooth, then store in refrigerator until needed.

INDEX